SNEAKY PRESS
©Copyright 2022
Pauline Malkoun

The right of Pauline Malkoun to be identified as author of this work has been asserted by them in accordance with Copyright, Designs and Patents Act 1988.

All Rights Reserved.

No reproduction, copy or transmission of this publication may be made without written permission. No paragraph of this publication may be reproduced, copied or transmitted save with the written permission of the publisher, or in accordance with the provisions of the Copyright Act 1956 (as amended).

Any person who commits any unauthorized act in relation to this publication may be liable to criminal prosecution and civil claims for damages.

A catalogue record for this work is available from the National Library of Australia.

ISBN 9781922641229

Sneaky Press is the imprint of Sneaky Universe.
www.sneakyuniverse.com
First published in 2022

Sneaky Press
Melbourne, Australia.

Sneaky Jokes

Volume 1

Sneaky Press

Why are jokes great?

There are so many reasons that jokes are fabulous including the following:

⇒ Better overall health and wellbeing. Laughter is the best medicine—that's why there are clown doctors who treat sick children in hospitals.

⇒ Jokes provide opportunities to interact with others, building social skills.

⇒ Jokes help build literacy—reading, speaking, expanding vocabulary, identifying sounds, additional meanings and spelling.

⇒ Jokes help build coping skills. They give us an outlet when we are faced with a tough situation—laughing at a joke can help relieve stress.

What do birds give out at Halloween?

Tweets!

What event do spiders love attending?

Webbings.

How do you know when a bike is thinking?

You can see it's wheels turning.

What time is it when people are throwing pieces of bread at your head?

Time to duck.

What's the difference between a guitar and a fish?

You can tune a guitar but you can't tuna fish.

What is a snake's favourite subject at school?

Hiss-tory.

What type of music do mummies love listening to?

Wrap music.

Why don't you ever see elephants hiding in trees?

Because they are really good at it.

Why is it so windy inside a sports stadium?

There are thousands of fans.

Why couldn't the music teacher start his car?

His keys were on the piano.

Why didn't the lamp sink?

Because it was too light.

Why shouldn't you tell secrets in a cornfield?

There are too many ears.

Why do bowling pins have a hard life?

They are always getting knocked down.

Why did the golfer wear two pairs of trousers?

In case he got a hole in one.

Why can't zookeepers be trusted?

Because they love cheetahs.

Where do you learn to make ice-cream?

At sundae school.

Why did the tomato blush?

It saw the salad dressing.

What type of tree fits in your hand?

A palm tree.

What did the grandmother elephant say to her grandkids when they were misbehaving?

"Tusk, tusk."

Where can hamburgers go dancing?

At a meat ball.

What time is it when a ball breaks the window?

Time to get a new window.

What do you call a bear without teeth?

A gummy bear.

What did the traffic light say to the car?

"Don't look now. I'm about to change."

What do you call a sad strawberry?

A blue berry.

What happened with the kidnapping at the park?

They woke him up.

What's a skeleton's favourite musical instrument?

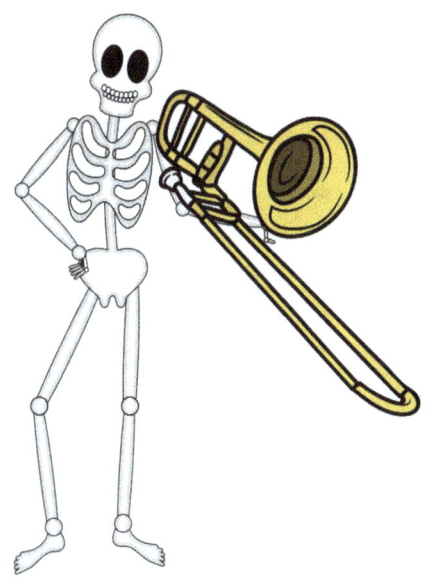

A trom—bone.

www.ingramcontent.com/pod-product-compliance
Lightning Source LLC
Chambersburg PA
CBHW050508120526
44588CB00044B/1852